CW00669622

A BOOT UP

THE SPEYSIDE WAY

Heidi M. Sands

First published in Great Britain in 2010

British Library Cataloguing-in-Publication Data
A CIP record for this title is available from the British Library

ISBN 978 1 906887 91 9

PiXZ Books
Halsgrove House, Ryelands Industrial Estate,
Bagley Road, Wellington, Somerset TA21 9PZ
Tel: 01823 653777
Fax: 01823 216796
email: sales@halsgrove.com

An imprint of Halstar Ltd, part of the Halsgrove group of companies
Information on all Halsgrove titles is available at: www.halsgrove.com

Printed and bound in China by Toppan Leefung Printing Ltd

Contents

How to use this book

A couple of years ago, quite by chance, I met one of the most inspiring men I've ever come across. Jacques Abdelaziz was walking the Speyside Way, but not as so many of us do, from one end at Aviemore to the other at Spey Bay, but from his home in Brittany, France. Not only did he do it all on foot but he had two of the most unusual companions such a walker could have, his donkeys, mother and daughter Nou Nou and Tou Toune. I met up with him mid way along the Speyside Way at Craigellachie. As we sat and conversed in broken English the two donkeys grazed the grass around us, resting and enjoying the hospitality that the wardens there lavished on them. It made me feel humble; the walk of this unusual threesome had taken in the crossing of the Forth Road Bridge at Edinburgh on hoof and foot alongside exceptionally heavy traffic.

On the Speyside Way their walk was much calmer and quieter and it is this calm and quiet that many of us seek as an antidote to our own Forth Road Bridges.

The Speyside Way is approximately 80 miles in total, it has been extended from its original length and there are plans to extend it further from Aviemore to Newtonmore. A large part of it is along the old Strathspey railway line and if you look there are still signs along the way of bridges, platforms and the most fantastic tunnel approaching Craigellachie from Aberlour. But it is the accessibility that the Speyside Way affords to other gems in the area that makes this path worth traversing. Just off the Speyside Way there is much to see, both unique sights and national treasures. The Telford Bridge at Craigellachie, possibly the most photographed bridge in the north east of Scotland is a magnificent sight and well worth the detour from the Speyside Way. As is the Macallan distillery at Elchies, and it is these and other gems that this little volume seeks to uncover and explore.

Using the Speyside Way as its starting point, this book takes in 10 walks, on, along and deviating off, the Speyside Way, each with a point, or in some cases several points, of interest to see. Some walks offer the opportunity to see the wildlife of the area, the dolphins at Spey Bay if you are lucky, the chance to camp out under the stars, as Jacques Abdelaziz did with his donkeys, or to rest peacefully in one of the excellent establishments along the way. Most of the walks are not too long and are suitable for families with older children. One though, to Loch Spey deserves a special mention, it is a walk for the more experienced and only to be undertaken with careful consideration; mobile phones do not work here and it is possible to be alone for hours with nothing more than deer and sheep as companions. Such areas can be dangerous, travel only with another walker and always leave your route and expected return time with someone; your life may depend on it.

With a spur off the Speyside Way to Tomintoul, the highest village in the Highlands, the walker is literally following in the footsteps of the ancient cattle drovers. Queen Victoria passed through and much of the scenery remains unchanged since she was there. The village itself has at times been home to colourful characters, whisky smugglers and illegal small scale distilleries peppered the area.

At nearby Glenlivet the walker has the chance to sample whisky legally and enjoy the walk to the pack horse bridge.

Part of the Speyside Way runs through the newly established Cairngorms National Park. Walkers experience heather hills and pine forests with the chance of roe or red deer sightings and maybe osprey soaring overhead or fishing in the Spey. Throughout the seasons you can never quite be certain what you'll come across in this most natural of places, nor what the weather will throw at you.

Resplendent in a warm autumn glow and alive with wild summer flowers the Way can offer something totally different when clothed in a snowy mantel. Farmland and livestock must be respected and understanding given to those who live and work here, value what they impart to you, dogs must be kept on leads at all times and others including horse and bicycle riders considered. Make sure that you are kitted out with sufficient regard for possible weather changes, no matter how easy a walk may seem on the surface never forget that Speyside can experience all kinds of weather on one day. Never be complacent and make sure your boots fit well, for there is nothing worse than ill fitting boots. Ensure that you carry an OS map and compass and know how to use them, be sure that someone has a good idea of where you are walking and your approximate return time. Above all take care, enjoy yourself along the Speyside Way, never be afraid to turn back nor to return again.

I used Harvey's XT40 Speyside Way map for all walks except that to Loch Spey where the OS Map 401 Explorer series was used (Loch Laggan and Creag Meagaidh).

Useful websites

Harvey's Maps www.harveysmaps.co.uk
Speyside Way visitor centre
www.moray.gov.uk/area/speyway/webpages/index.htm

Public transport

www.spiritofspeyside.com
Greater Speyside ww.greaterspeyside.com
Visit Scotland www.visitscotland.com
SNH/recreation www.outdooraccess-scotland.com

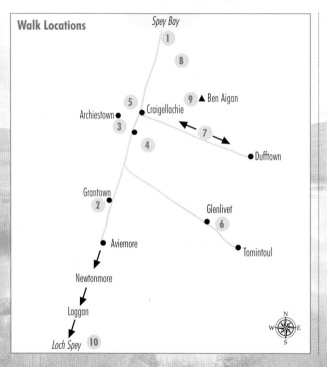

Walk Locations

Spey Bay

(1)

(8)

(5)   ▲ Ben Aigan

(9)

Archiestown ●   ● Craigellachie

(3)

(4)   (7)

● Dufftown

Grantown

(2)   Glenlivet

(6)

Aviemore   ● Tomintoul

Newtonmore

Laggan

Loch Spey (10)

Key to Symbols Used

Level of difficulty:
Easy
Moderate
More Challenging

Map symbols:

🚗	Park & start
——	Tarred Road
– – –	Footpath
	River, stream or brook
■	Building
+	Church
▲	Triangulation pillar or other landmark
🚻	WC
🍴	Refreshments
🍺	Pub

Spey Bay

A coastal jaunt with beautiful sea views across the Moray Firth with time to marvel at the Spey Viaduct.

Spey Bay is a special place at any time of the year. Osprey fish where the River Spey empties into the sea and bottlenose dolphins are often seen during the summer months. The dolphins can be viewed from the shingle beach and the wildlife centre at Spey Bay is heavily involved in their protection. Other species visit too including harbour porpoises and minke whales. Basking sharks have been seen along the coast along with a huge variety of sea birds including cormorant, oystercatchers, goldeneye ducks and mergansers. It may be difficult to pull yourself away from the shore to begin this walk!

Level:
Length: 2½ miles
Terrain: Well defined paths, which may be slippery when wet.
Park and start: From outside the WDCS Wildlife Centre at Spey Bay. Seasonal opening with facilities. (GR NJ 350 656)
Website: www.wdcs.org/wildlifecentre

Tugnet

Spey Bay

River Spey

Viaduct

Contemplating the next stretch of the walk.

Ben Rinnes in the far distance with the viaduct closer.

(1) Leave the car park via the beach, taking the little wooden bridge at the side of the domed Ice House. Ben Rinnes and Ben Aigan are visible in the far distance, nearer and to your right is the viaduct we are heading to.

(2) Keep to the well defined path along the side of the Spey itself. Here there are good views back

The Speyside Way marker.

up towards Speyside. If you turn around you can often see seabirds from here, resting on the islets and islands in the bay. Underfoot can be slippery so take care. Head through trees before turning right onto a wider path walking alongside farmland.

(3) Meander pleasantly along ignoring the first track on the right that heads towards the river and continue on. The farmland opens out and a farm track cuts across in front of you and heads left; keep on following the Speyside Way marker.

The reserve sign.

4 On meeting the blue Spey Bay Wildlife Reserve sign keep on the tarmaced piece which is the Aberdeen to Inverness Moray section of the National Cycle Network. This is the crossing point.

5 Turn right onto the cycle way through the trees and the Spey soon becomes visible on your left as you get your first glimpse of the viaduct itself. Himalayan balsam proliferates hereabouts in season. The viaduct is a magnificent structure spanning the river. A lattice work of iron beneath which flows a torrent of water, the central section of the bridge arches upwards in a semi-circle. Underneath in the middle of the river is a large shingle and sand spit with washed up flotsam and jetsam in the form of rooted trees from recent storms. Take a look out to sea or back inland towards Ben Rinnes.

The viaduct was opened in 1886 by the Great North of Scotland railway. The original bridge was designed by Joseph Mitchell and was replaced in 1906 by the structure you see today. It was built to carry the Elgin to Buckie section of the railway.

6 After inspection of the bridge return back to the junction of the Speyside Way and the cycle track. Retracing your steps, take the first track off the Speyside Way on your right. This track between arable fields takes you to the road.

The wildlife centre.

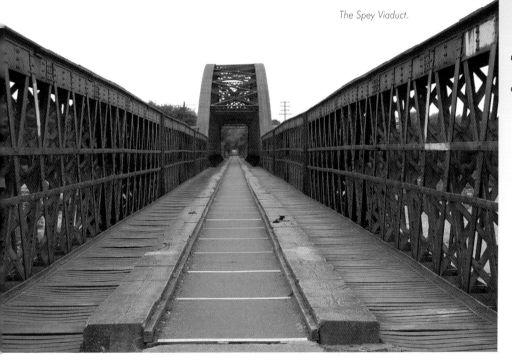

The Spey Viaduct.

11

(7) Turn left at this point heading towards the Spey Bay hotel and the coastline. On reaching the hotel turn back towards the Wildlife Centre car park and tea room for a welcome cup of tea.

The osprey sculpture near the car park.

2 **Grantown on Spey**

A walk around the outskirts of Grantown on Spey with some spectacular views, through woodland and by the River Spey.

Grantown on Spey is a beautiful place, world renowned for its connection with the river that flows close by, a salmon river that fishermen seek out, revere and return to year after year. Grantown is however more than somewhere to lay your head once the day is over. It has history for which a visit to the museum is a must, walks – one of which you might just follow me on – and a truly warm welcome to all who seek it out.

Level: 🥾🥾

Length: Approx 4 miles

Terrain: On good paths, with some steep sections that can be muddy. Quiet minor road and short section alongside the A95.

Park and start: Turn off Grantown on Spey's main street at the Garth Hotel into Burnfield Avenue car park. Free parking and toilets across from the town's museum.

Website/info: Grantown Museum
www.grantownmuseum.co.uk
Start GR NJ 011 289
Revack Estate Tel. 01479 872234

The view from the Spey Road Bridge.

1 Leaving the museum head away from the main street and at the bottom of the road turn left, reaching the golf course, turn right and walk through the golf green to a little wooden gate into Anagach Wood.

2 Take the little slip path in front of you and join the Speyside Way at the thistle marker, turn right to follow the path which is steep and can be muddy in places, through pretty woodland, and cross a couple of small streams.

3 Walking into the open by the thistle marker you enter the woods again. Stay on the main path, pass through a gate by a car park and continue ahead to a green finger sign post, here take a left towards Nethybridge.

Grantown's bell in the grounds of the museum.

Anagach Woods.

cross the road here and take a better look at the river if you have the inkling, before turning left along the quiet minor road. You are now on the Strathspey estate. Heading towards the Old Spey Bridge you pass a beautiful row of old stone houses. Keep on, ignoring two left turns, past the Strathspey estate office (imagine working here with such

(4) Passing through another gateway onto a wide thistle marked trail well used by other walkers and users, here you are in a stunning area of beech woods. Two stone pillars guide you on and later a wooden seat bids you rest and contemplate.

(5) You can hear the great river Spey before you actually see it. Coming out of the woods you can

Cyclists in the woods.

6 Leaving the bridge turn right by the memorial stone to the Honourable Lord Charles Hay opposite the imposing Speybridge House. Heading towards the main road pass through a gate. At this point turn round to see cottages and crofts synonymous with the area before crossing the main road in front of the smokehouse.

The Old Spey Bridge.

a view as the staff must have) and onto the Old Spey Bridge. Stop a while to savour the views in both directions. The Spey valley opens out before you and while fishermen and women avail themselves of the bounty in the water consider the farmers in the fields and the gamekeepers and stalkers out on the hills.

Each year in early August Grantown holds its annual Strathspey Farmers' Club show in Heathfield Park. Established in 1787 the gathering showcases some of the best livestock the area has to offer. From Highland cattle to Highland ponies, Blackfaced sheep and Clydesdale heavy horses the spectator is left in no doubt as to the importance that the native breeds have in the area.

One of Grantown on Spey's delightful stone cottages.

(7) For those who wish to visit, Revack Estate welcomes visitors; this is a short walk further along the road off which the smokehouse is entered.

The Hay memorial by the Old Spey Bridge.

(8) The return to Grantown is partly along the A95, here to the right. At the newer road bridge over the river Spey stop and savour yet more river views, before reaching the roundabout.

The River Spey.

(9) Here you have a choice. Either take the exit signposted to the Old Spey Bridge and continue until you pick up the Anagach woodland path on your left retracing your route back to the museum or, for those who like to browse, continue on and into Grantown itself. Turn right when you reach the High Street, do your browsing, continue into the Square and at the far end of the road by the Garth Hotel turn right back into Burnfield Avenue.

3 **Archiestown Village**

A walk around Archiestown, a picturesque village square and a stretch through wooded countryside.

Level:
Length: 2 miles approximately
Terrain: Mostly peaceful level village lanes with a stretch of good forest track.
Park and start: In front of the Archiestown Hotel in the centre of the village, the hotel provides accommodation and good food. (GR NJ 230 445)
Websites: Archiestown Hotel
www.archiestownhotel.co.uk
Furniture makers www.gvis.co.uk/ballintomb-furniture

Archiestown village boasts a beautiful village square where old properties mingle with new and restored cottages sit alongside the village hall and the old manse. Frequently Moray's best kept village the summer flower arrangements are quite stunning and show just why the village has had such acclaim. Sitting in the centre of the square is the war memorial to the men of Knockando parish. Just outside the village is the home of Burnside of Ballintomb furniture makers, well worth a visit – take the Knockando road for approximately half a mile, it is well signed.

Archiestown war memorial in the village square.

19

There are some very old buildings within the village.

1 Leave the hotel by South Lane at the bottom end of the car park, proceed passing farm buildings within the village boundary. There are far-reaching views to Ben Rinnes on your right and there is much to delight the eye. Take your time to peep over garden walls and

Archiestown paths.

explore the tiny lanes that offshoot towards the High Street. This is a leisurely walk with interest for the whole family. So much of the village is as it was 100 years ago and its formal layout is easy to follow.

2 Amble along to the end of the lane passing stables to your left and more open views on your right, rounding the corner by the impressive cream-boarded Rose Villa with its turret like entrance.

Continue and cross over the High Street where you leave Smiddy Lane for Schoolhouse Lane.

(3) Proceed along here, passing the entrance to North Lane and turning right into the playing field, perfect for those with young children. If joining the designated village walk tempts you, you can join it here, but we will return this way later in the walk. For now we will rejoin North Lane and proceed uphill towards a large Monkey Puzzle tree in the garden of Woodlea, before ending up at the upper end of the enchanting village square.

(4) Alongside the house known as Old St Andrews, North Lane meets the exit of the aforementioned

Archiestown frequently gets heavy winter snows and can be under feet of the white stuff. Streets have to be snow ploughed leaving a single trackway through for vehicles. Children are excused school and neighbours help one another in this traditional community, a rare something in this day and age.

The Old Manse in the village square.

village walk. Here there are several options, you can either cut the walk short by returning to the car park situated to your left or join the village walk to your right, which is what we will do.

(5) Proceed along here passing cottages and open farmland with the wind turbines on Ballindalloch Estate clearly visible. Turn right onto the next track which may be wet at certain times. There are far reaching views of Ben Rinnes from the reservoir where there is a seat from which to appreciate the sight. Continue along the path and at the wooden gate in front of you take the path to the right downhill under the

rowan trees. Stay on this path, bearing right until you reach the aforementioned children's play park. There are often ponies here, a delight to behold.

6 Proceed to the High Street and turn right onto it, taking your time to take in the village's older buildings and named lanes; Craigroy, McQibbans, Bakers, Chapel, McGowans and Souters Lanes – all reminiscent of a bygone age.

7 Proceed up a flight of steps by the hotel where you can either take well-earned refreshment or return to your car. There is also a bus stop by the hotel for those who wish to use public transport.

The woodland section.

Archiestown village with the hills beyond.

4 **Aberlour**

Aberlour is one of the most beautiful settlements on Speyside and the perfect place to meander alongside the Spey, the Lour Burn and the Linn Falls.

Level: 🥾 (unsuitable for buggies)
Length: 2½ miles
Terrain: Off road paths, uphill section that may be wet.
Park and start: By the Victoria Bridge. (GR NJ 278 437)
Website/info: Facilities/amenities in Aberlour. The Mash Tun www.mashtun-aberlour.com

Aberlour is the jewel in Speyside's crown. Visitors flock there for the scenery, fishing and whisky trail. There's more to Aberlour than just tourism and the walk we are to do takes in much of the village's history. From the Alice Littler Park where the walk begins history is all around you. Here the Strathspey Railway had its station in what is now the Speyside Way visitor centre. As the walk progresses you pass Aberlour's oldest structure, the pack horse bridge over the Lour Burn. The remains of the old Kirk of Skirdustan; the old name for Aberlour, stand close by. Further into the walk there's the chance to stop and admire the clock tower, all that remains of the old Aberlour Orphanage founded by Canon Jupp, and the commemorative garden to all the children who called Aberlour home. St Margaret's church completes this historical round.

Linn Falls

3

4

+ St Margaret's church

Aberlour Distillery

High Street

2

The Mash Tun

1

N
W E
S

River Spey

The Alice Littler Park at Aberlour.

1 Leaving the car park by the Victoria Bridge cross the pathway and go through the gate heading towards the new metal bridge over the Lour. Don't take this bridge but turn left alongside the burn. Stop at the old packhorse bridge, built in the early 1600s or peep over the wall into the cemetery. It's rumoured that Hare, one half of the infamous pair Burke and Hare, may be buried here.

(2) Cross the road in front of the Aberlour Distillery. Follow the sign for the Linn Falls, a beautiful walk passing ancient trees, the distillery and rushing water. There are several steep and stony sections. Keep on the main path until you reach the waterfall; dippers are often seen here. Once you've admired this unique place continue up the steps above the waterfall. Here are more steep sections with smaller falls of water. Keep to the central footpath where it splits into three through woodland, then take the left fork immediately after the bench, not through the wooden kissing gate, but onto a wider level path that takes you to the back of Aberlour.

Opposite: The Lour Burn.
Right: The Linn Falls.

3 Cross the car park for a splendid view across the village and the valley. Go through a gateway and turn left onto the road at Stac Pollaidh and continue downhill, nip through the trees on your left at the bottom and over a little bridge, crossing the road downhill. Continue, turn right into Mary Avenue, pass the school and turn right into Conval Drive, the clock tower of the Aberlour Orphanage cannot be missed. Under the arch is a brief history. Continue on through into the commemorative garden. Retrace your steps under the arch, turn right then left to follow the path under the trees.

The Clock Tower of Aberlour Orphanage.

The memorial garden to Aberlour Orphanage.

The Mash Tun.

(4) The path emerges at St Margaret's church. Here within the churchyard are tributes to the children and staff of Aberlour Orphanage. At the front of the church turn down the avenue and meet the High Street. Cross the road at Milford, turn right and walk the short distance to Riversyde, turn left along the wall to rejoin the Speyside Way. Turn left and look out for the unusually shaped Mash Tun public house on the left as you go through the park before reaching your car.

The walk back to the High Street.

St Margaret's churchyard holds several gems with memorials to William Grant of Wester Elchies and John Gillam White originator of a particular variety of large double Begonia.

5 Elchies

A country walk with the chance to sample some of the best malt whisky in the world, the Macallan.

Thomas Telford's bridge at Craigellachie is a huge draw to visitors. At night it is floodlit with lights trained on the rock that sits behind it and along which the old road runs. Although now closed to traffic locals remember the buses having to make three point turns in order to get round the tight bend on and off the bridge. When the bus driver was successful the passengers often let out a cheer, many larger vehicles didn't make it

Level:
Length: 4 miles
Terrain: Quiet country lanes, one busier section on the B9102. Good off road path.
Park and start: By the Telford Bridge at Craigellachie. (GR NJ 287 453)
Website/info: The Macallan www.themacallan.com
Booking advised for tours. All facilities in Aberlour.

cleanly, leaving tell tail paint on the rock wall; the bridge was of course built to take horse drawn traffic. On top of this great rock is the home of the Macallan Distillery. The bridge and the distillery have had long links, one making it easier for the other's wares to cross over the Spey.

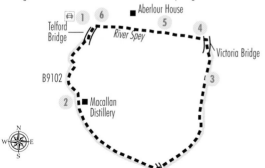

The Telford Bridge at Craigellachie.

At Wester Elchies.

1 Park beside the Telford Bridge and leave the car park by walking onto the bridge, taking in the view towards Ben Rinnes. Walk off the bridge along the old road, at the main road turn left along the pavement taking the little path uphill on your

At the entrance to the Macallan Distillery.

left. This may be overgrown but press on until you meet the B9102. Take care here, the road is twisty and climbs uphill, follow it to the Macallan Distillery entrance. It pays to book ahead for tours but the visitor centre is open to all and this walk would be incomplete without taking a look at where the amber nectar is made.

2 After taking a dram, rejoin the B9102 and walk on past the new distillery warehouses to a fork in the road by Overton House. Take the left fork to Ringorm and proceed down this quiet lane, over a bridge and uphill. The views from here are splendid, look to your left to see Aberlour House; once prep school for Gordonstoun

The view to Aberlour.

where many of our modern royal family have been educated. The road passes farmland before entering a stand of trees. Keep on at the right hand turn and drop down past the Wester Elchies fishing sign. Stay on the road through the estate. Keep on downhill ignoring the right turn, from here you overlook Aberlour.

3 Continue downhill and at the bottom turn left through the trees, the Spey becomes visible and the Victoria Bridge is in front of you. As you walk over the bridge keep a look

The Spey between Aberlour and Craigellachie.

out for salmon rising. The bridge will swing as you walk, don't be alarmed.

Much of the Speyside Way was once a busy railway. It transported people, livestock and raw materials for the whisky industry. Most of what remains of the railway is in the form of bridges and tunnels.

4 Leaving the bridge turn left into the Alice Littler Park and follow the river path. Here the Aberlour Games are held each summer. To your right as you walk is the old railway building, used by the Speyside Way rangers as their base and visitor centre, open seasonally.

Gardens at Aberlour.

5 Continue along the Speyside Way. The gardens here are extremely pretty, the Spey is on your left. Passing out of Aberlour continue towards Craigellachie where you approach the huge old railway tunnel through which you pass. Continue on into Craigellachie and at the back of the Highlander Inn turn left into the children's play park.

6 Walk through the playpark alongside the river and under the new road bridge that brings you back to where you started.

6 Glenlivet

The prettiest of walks, along quiet country roads, with the chance to sample the amber nectar at the Glenlivet Distillery and a packhorse bridge straight out of a fairy tale.

Level:
Length: 2 miles
Terrain: Mostly good country roads, some steep inclines, a stretch of grassy path, farm track and riverside walking.
Park and start: The Glenlivet Distillery (GR NJ 196 290)
Website/info: Glenlivet Distillery www.glenlivet.com Tours and a dram.

This walk is a real gem, my personal favourite in the book and steeped in history. Partake of a tour at the distillery

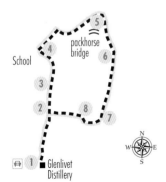

before you begin, or later on your return from the walk; possibly a better idea as a welcome repast, instead of a drunken doddle if you top up first, so to speak! This is the 'high tops' in terms of weather and could be cold and inclement, so come prepared with hats, gloves and good footwear. The views are spectacular, the river beautiful, and the packhorse bridge a real find; all that and whisky too. This is a hill farming area and snow comes early

here and lies long. Cattle are brought inside for the winter and lambing is delayed until the better spring weather arrives. However sudden spring storms can catch the farmer out and losses can be high in a bad spell.

The Speyside Way marker at Glenlivet Distillery.

1 Leave the car park through the distillery, following the road. The smell is both delicious and intoxicating — yum! A promise for later. Sometimes doors are open giving you a peep into the industry. Very pretty grounds with running water, ducks and ornamental planting guide you to a way marker of the Speyside Way with the thistle mark. It's very quiet here even though you are on the road, a pastoral scene with horses, sheep and cattle grazing. There are far reaching views past Minmore farmhouse with Ben Rinnes in the far distance with its distinctive long low climb on the left contrasting with a steeper right hand ascent topped with granite outcrop.

Glenlivet Distillery beneath vast skies.

Minmore House and buildings.

(4) Turn right before the Give Way sign missing out part of the road in favour of a little path that takes you over the river, a fantastic sight when in spate. Continue to the bus stop by the graveyard and look out for herons that are sometimes to be seen fishing here. Rejoin the road and bear right towards Tomintoul signed 9 miles. If you have time visit the graveyard. 150 yards further on is the packhorse bridge at Bridgend of Glenlivet.

A welcome to Bridgend of Glenlivet.

(2) Just beyond the entrance to Minmore House the thistle sign indicates right, downhill. Ignore this and carry on, you will return this way. Here a sign on your left encourages you to follow George Smith's smugglers trail on the Crown Estate but we are not going that way.

(3) There are super views as you descend the road, this is real hill country, the river and packhorse bridge may be just visible as you reach the school building, (imagine coming to school here, surrounded by so much history and beauty).

The packhorse bridge.

5 The prettiest of walks, long low cottages hug the roadside here. Enter the car park on your right to admire the double humped packhorse bridge over the Livet. Picnic tables encourage you to stop and appreciate the scene. Return to the road and continue right, around the curve. The river here is absolutely beautiful and very dramatic, but don't get too close. Pass the aptly named 'Falls Cottage', bypassing beautiful woodland at any time of the year but especially so in the autumn with wonderfully rich colours.

Originally three arches the packhorse bridge at Glenlivet had its third arch swept away in 1829. Probably built by the owner of Blairfindy Castle during the 16th century, the bridge was rescued by Moray Council who began a programme of repairs and restoration work in 1985. Today floods still reach well up the river and are capable of doing damage.

6 Continue on to Glenlivet Hall where a notice informs you that camping and caravaning are allowed. By the bridge there pick up the Speyside Way again, thistle marked between road and river. Go over the stile and turn left onto a grassy track.

One of Glenlivet's cottages.

Here part of the bank has been undercut by the river, take care and continue over a little footbridge. This is a lovely riverside walk. Follow the route marker thistle down onto a sandy path that could be difficult when wet. Pass Minmore Walk 6 circular disc in a tree and close by the thistle marker encourages you onward, towards a substantial bridge over the river to your right.

(7) Go over the bridge and continue, closing the gate on the end of the bridge to prevent livestock following you over. A plaque on the bridge tells you the 2nd Troop of the 104 City of Edinburgh Field Squadron RE(V) built the bridge in 1983. Below you a ford is clearly visible, and although wired the bridge may be slippery when wet.

The Livet.

(8) Here you enter the National Park, follow the way marker to your right uphill, the distillery comes into view on your left. Turn left at the end of the road and return to the car park. A truly splendid walk for very little effort.

Right on the edge of the Cairngorms National Park.

7 Dufftown

A tree-lined river walk steeped in railway and whisky history. This is a linear walk, combined with public transport.

Level:
Length: 4 miles
Terrain: Level stone path.
Park and start: Park at the Fiddich car park at Craigellachie. Toilet facilities in the park are seasonal April – October. Camping allowed in the park. Start the walk proper after a short bus ride to the Glenfiddich Distillery at Dufftown. Start GR NJ 324 411
Info: Hotels/shop at Craigellachie.
www.whiskyinn.com
Shops/tea room/accommodation and TIC (seasonal) at Dufftown.
Bus times www.stagecoachbus.com/bluebird

The path from Dufftown to Craigellachie was until a couple of years ago a second spur – after Tomintoul, – of the Speyside Way. Recent damage to the path by landslides has caused it to be downgraded and it's no longer officially part of the Way. However the path remains and is a good walk in spite of care needed on the landslip section. This is a linear walk utilising public transport, I've chosen to walk from Dufftown to Craigellachie; but you could do it the other way, simply because the path descends in that direction, it also seems natural to follow the River Fiddich in the direction that it flows. Doing it this way you can spend time in Dufftown before you

begin the walk, or enjoy the trains at Dufftown Station. Even out of season you can meander along the platform marvelling at Pullman carriages and the like. It's a feast for the enthusiast.

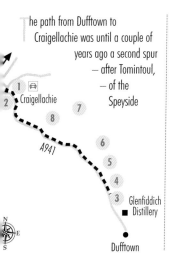

1
Craigellachie
2
8
7
A941
6
5
4
3 Glenfiddich
■ Distillery

Dufftown

N
W   E
S

43

Dufftown's clock tower.

1 Leave the car park via steps up to the village, in the trees along the continuation of the track you took down to the car park from the road. Turn left at the top of the steps and walk to the end of the road. Turn right, then left at the bottom of the road and onto the petrol station to wait for the Bluebird bus.

2 A 5-minute bus ride takes you either to the Glenfiddich Distillery or into Dufftown for a look around before retracing your steps back to the distillery where the walk begins. Avail yourself of the tours at the Glenfiddich first if you are keen; it's one of the most famous distilleries in the world. From the bus stop retrace your steps away from Dufftown along the road passing between the distillery

Trains at Dufftown.

warehouses. Note the blackened bark of the trees caused by the whisky process, it occurs at most distilleries. Continue on to Dufftown Station.

(3) Walk onto the platform at the green finger sign post and turn left along the platform signed to the Isla Way. Linger even if you are not enraptured by rail travel. The ticket office still has it's wooden interior and the station clock and post box from George VI's reign survive. Press on along the platform to your left and at the end of the track take the footpath to Craigellachie with the Balvenie Distillery on your right.

(4) Cross the road into the trees. You are on the Dufftown/ Loch Park section of the Isla Way for a short distance. Going over the first in a series of railway bridges, you pass the

Glenfiddich Distillery.

pagoda tops of the distillery, then through a gate with a sign reminding you of the landslip further on. Continue to bridge 233 and over a road bridge. A green finger sign takes others to Loch Park and Drummuir, but we continue on with more bonded warehouses on the right.

(5) Walk through birch trees and the River Fiddich comes into view. The sound of water will accompany you to Craigellachie. Storm damaged trees lie to the left in gullies that empty water into the river and roe are often seen hereabouts.

The tops of whisky buildings peep through the trees.

Country cottages along the way.

7 The river crosses in front of you and under your path as you walk over bridge 240, then another larger bridge with lovely river views. Pass between more rocky outcrops. The river is now on your left. The path descends and crosses another railway bridge, now fenced. A second fenced area takes you through more woods and over another railed bridge.

Dappled light along the way.

6 Continue through the trees and Kininvie House is visible on your right, shortly after you arrive at the landslide, signed for caution, do be careful, it's passable without too much trouble. The path continues under the trees and curves to your left as you cross another railway bridge, before heading between two rocky outcrops.

No two whiskies are the same and it is said that Speyside whisky is the best in the world. The industry has a language all of its own. From 'washbacks' to 'pagodas', 'bonds', 'mashing', 'grist' and 'wort' it's well worth taking in at least one distillery tour on a visit to Speyside.

8 You are now above a wider river basin and come to a stone wall on your left, the river disappears and you are between two more rocky outcrops. The remains of two large stone walls are either side of the path and you emerge onto a gated lane over the river. Proceed into the Fiddich park.

This is whisky country.

8 **Fochabers**

A woodland walk with river sections and a chance to view the outskirts of this lovely town.

Level: 🐾 (Unsuitable for buggies)
Length: 4 miles
Terrain: Off road path that can be muddy/wet. Paved sections.
Park and start: At the Fochabers Bicentenary Park off the A96. (GR NJ 342 593)
Website/info: Facilities and shops in Fochabers. www.baxters.com

Fochabers has been home to a number of outstanding people. From eminent physicians to the Baxter family of food fame, this small country town has old boys and girls who have taken their respective talents across the world. Fochabers has recognised their achievements with a Commemorative Garden and magnificent viewpoint overlooking the Spey. This garden is well worth a visit and is only a short stride into the walk we are to undertake. This is a walk for taking with the family dog, if you

have one. The woods are a dogs' delight with sniffs and undergrowth galore. If you don't have a dog do not be deterred, it's a twisty walk with something new to see almost around every corner. If variety is called for between countryside and town this is the walk for you.

The Crown Estate's information board at Fochabers Bicentenary Park.

1 From the car park take the path alongside the beech hedge, the Speyside Way thistle marker shows the way. Pass the cricket ground on your left with the Spey on your right. Here stop to admire the river from the view point garden with its remembrance stones to the men and women of Fochabers.

2 Drop down through the garden to the Speyside Way marker and the wooden footbridge over the burn. Cross the bridge. A paved road takes you to a junction and property including Harwood and Lochalsh. Keep straight on here and ignore a track up to your left. Go through the wood and a few hundred yards further on is a green finger sign post. Continue on ignoring the sign to your right.

Through the trees another finger post turns you left signed Fochabers Square; proceed through the trees to a burn.

Left: One of the large memorial stones for famous residents of Fochabers overlooking the Spey at the viewpoint.

Opposite: One of the many finger posts along the path.

3 At the Speyside Way marker ignore the steps in front of you and turn right onto an indistinct path. This can be wet and muddy, take care if so and walk on to a good grass path by the side of the burn and up a flight of wooden steps. You are now in open farmland with good views across the fields. Follow the path to newer properties and an older traditional cottage. Ignore the right turn following the Speyside Way marker and instead keep left over the burn. A quiet country lane takes you past Pennyland and Brooklands on your left. Ignore the Forestry Commission mountain bike trail entrance at

Fochabers is home to Baxters food group. You can visit them on the A96, a stone's throw from the Bicentenary Park. Step back in time to when George Baxter opened his grocer's shop in 1868 and enjoy their fine foods and specialities.

Ordiequish and keep straight on bypassing the next green finger sign post into Slorach's Wood. Keep on to the end of the lane just at the edge of town. There is another green finger sign post, take the left signed to Fochabers Square, The Intake and Community Walks and car park. The path runs between hedged

Forestry Commission mountain bike trails signs at Ordiequish.

Pastoral views.

farmland and school playing fields to another green finger sign post. Turn right between school and homes and head to the gate. Pass through where there is another marker by the Spey road sign. Head straight on by the mini roundabout. You are now on pavement by the side of the road. Continue and in front of the school another sign post points straight on. On passing the Old Manse and the Lodge on your right proceed and cross the weak bridge.

(4) Ignoring the right hand finger post sign, take the next left path beside the burn. At the next finger post sign continue on to the Memorial Garden and the Spey before returning to your car.

Somewhere to sit and enjoy the views.

9 Ben Aigan

A hill walk with the best and most complete 360 degree view for miles.

The walk up Ben Aigan is worth it for the views: it should rightly have been dubbed the 'Five Counties', for it's possible to see from the Sutherland Hills in the north across to Aberdeenshire, by way of The Black Isle in Ross and Cromarty, the Moray Firth in Morayshire and Banffshire. Turn south

Level: 🥾 🥾
Length: 9 miles
Terrain: Minor public road. Hill and forestry tracks.
Height achieved: Ben Aigan 471m (1546 ft) (GR NJ310 482)
Park and start: Fiddich car park, Craigellachie. Toilets/seasonal, camping allowed in the park.
Website: The Highlander Inn, Craigellachie www.whiskyinn.com

on the summit and Ben Rinnes fills the skyline. This is not only a place for walkers, it's a huge draw for mountain bikers. For this reason it pays to take care on the sections designated for biking; for the connoisseurs of the mountain bike world come thick and fast at times.

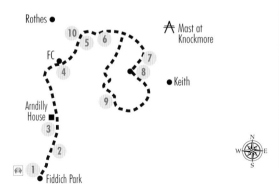

Taking in the view from the top with Ben Rinnes the highest point on view.

1. Leave the car park at the Fiddich by way of the finger post signed to Fochabers. Cross the road, bear right over the bridge and turn directly left by the sign to Arndilly and the Speyside Way marker. Proceed uphill with the River Fiddich on your left where it empties into the Spey. From here look out over Dandaleith as you work your way through Arndilly estate woodland. Pigeons roost here, red squirrels literally squirrel their food away and buzzards are often seen.

Arndilly House was once home to the McDowall Grant family. Built in 1750 it later caught fire and was destroyed. Rebuilt in 1770 it has since been added to.

2. Ignore the first road on your right and cross the stone bridge over the deep and wooded burn. Note the bridge's two smaller arches high up on either side of the main arch. The road bends; ignore the turning to Tominachty as Arndilly House comes into view on your left above the river. Continue amongst the trees. Ignoring all turns off this road, cross over a culvert with a single wall on your left, carry on towards Arndilly House, passing Arndilly fishing sign and over the bridge.

Looking down on the mast.

(3) Arndilly House is in front with the Speyside Way marker pointing the direction to take. Continue on and the road meanders until you see Rothes on your left.

(4) Shortly after you come to the Forestry Commission Ben Aigan sign. There's officially no parking

Tree roots in the likeness of a dog.

but don't be surprised to see vehicles. This is the access for mountain bikers and the Speyside Way. Go through the gate and the view is of Orton and Rothes. Walk on through Scots pine and larch until the Speyside Way marker appears as you meet the main track in front of you. Join this track to your left above the waterfall.

(5) The track swings round and past the roots of a tree that look for all the world like a dog sitting up with a stick in its mouth. Walk on to the sign post on your right 'Moray Monster Trails Ben Aigan Mountain Bike Trails', a rougher path than you have been on. Turn onto this and proceed uphill between the trees. This

section is quite steep. If you turn the view is splendid with the wind turbines on Rothes Estate visible on the skyline. On your left is Ben Rinnes, a second set of wind turbines sit at Paul's Hill, Ballindalloch Estate.

6 At the top of this section is another marker, 17 The Hammer, keep on, you are now on rough grass. As you climb the trees thin

and you emerge onto a heather covered plateau. There are far reaching views, to your left the TV transmitter mast at Knockmore, distillery warehouses at Mulben and Keith in the distance. Walk further, turn and you can see the Spey making its way to the coast.

7 Take the stony path to your right to the first shoulder of the hill. Here you can see the Black Isle,

Moray, Banff and Aberdeenshire. You are in the open, trees are stunted and mosses and lichens grow. A stone track leads to the summit and the OS point.

8 On reaching the top enjoy far reaching views. If you root about in the stones at the bottom of the OS marker there is a tin box, used as a visitors book, add your name and achievement and read those of others.

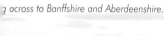
across to Banffshire and Aberdeenshire.

The top.

Mountain bikers

From the OS marker strike left with Ben Rinnes in front of you, off the top, down a path that gets clearer as you walk, it zigzags to a fork. In front is the forestry gateway to Mulben. Take the right hand path alongside the forestry. Go through the next gateway into the trees.

9 A pretty area of woodland is on your left, look down to a path below, drop down to join it where the

Hillwalking.

mountain bike sign indicates, 14 The Hammer, the Widow Maker and a skull and crossbones. Keep an eye out for mountain bikers hereabouts. Follow the trail. In places it's narrow with drops and ramps for bikers. Two more bike signs follow and ignore the forest track on your left. The path rises and falls several times. One last uphill spurt brings you to the earlier bike sign for The Hammer, a crossroads between hill and bike tracks. Turn left and retrace your steps to the main track. At the main track turn left.

10 Go down hill, round by the waterfall and take the next right to the Forestry Commission sign by the road. Turn left onto the road making your way back through the estate and the Fiddich car park.

10 Loch Spey

This is a largely linear walk, but it is none the worse for that, affording the walker a second chance to take in some of Scotland's most magnificent scenery.

Level: 🥾 🥾 🥾
Length: 15 miles
Terrain: Tarmac from Garva Bridge to Melgarve, from there to Loch Spey a rough hill track that in places deteriorates to nothing more than an indistinct deer path, wet in places.
Park and start: Park at Garva Bridge 3 miles from Laggan in Badenoch. (GR NH 522 948)
Info: Toilets and fully stocked shop at Laggan.

This is the toughest walk in the book, and if being truthful not on, or along the Speyside Way, but how could the walker traverse other sections of the great River Spey without venturing into the hills proper to see the source of one of Scotland's most famous salmon rivers, at Loch Spey. Make no mistake

this place is not for the fainthearted. It is not recommended that you undertake this walk in the winter – it is safely a summer walk best undertaken between April and October, be aware snow can fall even in June. Mobile phones do not work all along this route and it pays to walk with a

companion. Take a whistle in case you get stuck and do not be afraid to blow it in distress. Likewise be prepared to help others if the need arises. Don't be surprised to pass mountain bike enthusiasts along the way and horse riders from one of Scotland's longest trail rides regularly pass this way. Above all enjoy this spectacular place: it's one of the places to visit before old age and infirmity render it impossible.

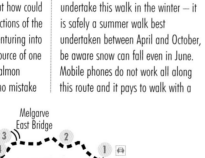

Leaving Garva Bridge after admiring the first of several bridges along the route head through the gate onto General Wade's military road. This ancient way, better known as the Corrieyairack Pass, begins by rising gently, with forestry to your left and hills on your right. Passing Creag Chathalain, two further plantations appear with Meall a' Ghiubhais towering overhead. Here the Spey is narrower and shallower than further downstream. Hill cows graze the peaty drainage basin and the road follows the line of electric pylons. Through more plantations of trees until the vista opens out and Melgarve comes into sight.

Above the river to your left Alltachorain bothy stands alone with its tumbling burn spilling down behind it into the Spey. As you approach Melgarve a sign to the right of the track by the sheep fold directs you to Melgarve East Bridge, a stunning single arch packhorse bridge, well worth the short detour along the wide grassy track

Garva Bridge.

General Wade's road.

The Corrieyairack Pass would, if still an adopted road today, be the highest in Britain; that it is not is good news for the walker. It was built to provide the most direct route between the Great Glen and Badenoch.

between the trees, just follow the sound of rushing water. Returning to the tarmac for a short time, head to Melgarve before the terrain changes to stone.

(3) Arrive at another packhorse bridge and a well appointed stone bothy, enter and avail yourself of its shelter but leave it as you found it, others may need the roof over their

Melgarve East Bridge.

The bothy at Melgarve.

heads more than you do and bolt the door to stop sheep from entering. There are glorious views looking back the way you came.

4 From the bothy take the left hand fork downhill, past Drummin and through the heavy duty metal gate. Keep to the stony track after a while bearing left around a stand of trees. Ignore the footbridge to your left keeping along the side of the trees. Cross the next bridge.

5 You now follow the line of trees and the infant Spey through peaceful bog grazing with magnificent views all around. Ford a small burn and continue. Keep your eyes peeled for red deer. At the end of the trees a building comes into view and here the Spey is little more than a meander. Cross over a footbridge just before the entrance to the aforementioned building.

The bridge at Melgarve.

The great River Spey begins life as a much smaller water source.

6 To your left there is an indistinct path on grass, take this path with care, over open moorland, this is not well used, is soft in places and deserves respect. Crossing several burns, the path gets fainter and boggier in places. Keep the infant river in sight traversing with care. The going improves with a disused summer sheiling on your right. Cross a wider stony-bottomed burn.

7 Head uphill to your right, skirting the wetter section ahead until Loch Spey comes into view. An open area set within the hills, it pays to allow some time to savour this wild place. Few others pass this way, more red deer frequent the area than people. Words alone cannot do this place justice.

Loch Spey as the clouds roll in.

8 Head back the way you came, taking in the atmosphere and views for a second time. Allow enough time and daylight for your return stint.

Homeward bound.